Intermediate through Early

SUCCEEDING WITH THE MASTERS®

BAROQUE ERA, Volume Two

Compiled and edited by Helen Marlais

About the Series

Succeeding with the Masters® is a series dedicated to the authentic keyboard works of the Baroque, Classical, Romantic, and Twentieth-Century masters.

This series provides a complete and easily accessible method for learning and performing the works of the masters. Each book presents the works in historical perspective for the student, and provides the means and the motivation to play these pieces in the correct stylistic, musical, and technical manner. The easily understandable format of practice strategies and musical concepts make this series enjoyable for both students and teachers.

To ensure authenticity, all of these pieces have been extensively researched. Teachers will find a wealth of excellent repertoire that can be used for recitals, festivals, competitions, and state achievement testing. Many of these original compositions may be new to you while others will be familiar. This series brings together an essential and comprehensive library of the pedagogical repertoire of the great composers.

Succeeding with the Masters® begins with late-elementary repertoire, continues through intermediate-level works and also includes a few early-advanced works. Upon completion of this series, students will be well prepared for the entry-level sonatas by the master composers.

THE
F·J·H
MUSIC
COMPANY
INC.
Frank J. Hackinson

Production: Frank J. Hackinson
Production Coordinators: Philip Groeber and Isabel Otero Bowen
Cover: Terpstra Design, San Francisco – in collaboration with Helen Marlais
Cover: Chalk lithograph of J. S. Bach from the *Pougin Iconography Collection*, Sibley Music Library.
Text Design and Layout: Susan Pinkerton
Engraving: Tempo Music Press, Inc.
Printer: Tempo Music Press, Inc.

ISBN-13: 978-1-56939-480-9

PREFACE

A Note for Teachers and Students

Succeeding with the Masters®, Baroque Era Volume Two, continues the collection of graded repertoire featuring the great masters of the Baroque era. Volume Two includes intermediate-level and early advanced pieces. This collection of marvelous repertoire builds a foundation for playing even more advanced baroque music. After studying and performing these pieces, the student will be ready for the two-part inventions by Bach and the more difficult Scarlatti sonatas and Handel suites. Each piece is introduced with a short "discovery" of a particular characteristic of the Baroque era. Brief segments on "practice strategies" guide the student in how to prepare and perform the piece. This comprehensive approach to learning style, technique, and historical context provides a valuable foundation for successful performance of all baroque repertoire pieces.

Two icons are used throughout the volume:

Characteristics of the Baroque Era

indicates the Musical Characteristics of the Baroque era.

Practice Strategy

outlines a practice strategy or illustrates a musical concept that guides the student in how to learn more efficiently and play more musically.

Many published collections take liberties in altering pitches, rhythms, and articulations that the composers clearly did not intend. The pieces in this collection, however, are based on facsimiles of the composer's own manuscripts, and on Urtext editions, which are editions that reflect the composer's original intent. The Scarlatti sonatas are based on two sets of manuscripts made by copyists, called the Venice and Parma manuscripts. From these manuscripts, the editor has created performance scores for the student.

- Since the composers did not supply dynamic markings or fingerings, please note that all of the dynamics and fingerings are editorial, and are intended as a guide for students as they explore the baroque style.
- In a few cases, editorial markings are added to help guide the student. These markings are identified with *N.B.* or an * and accompanied by a footnote so that teacher and student know exactly what appears in the original score.
- Editorial metronome markings are added as a guide.
- Ornaments have been realized for the student and appear as ossias above the staff.
- The downloadable recordings include complete performances and a practice strategy workshop. For a complete listing of track numbers, see page six.

MUSIC DURING THE BAROQUE ERA (1600–1750)

The early Baroque period was one of the most revolutionary in music history. The first opera was performed in Florence, Italy, and musicians began to think very differently about both melody and harmony and about how music could dramatically express emotion. In the middle phase of the baroque (1640–1680), new musical styles spread from Italy to all of Europe, placing importance on instrumental music rather than vocal music. One new feature was *basso continuo*, or "continuous bass" which composers used to support the structure of the music. Another was *affect*, the concept of expressing a specific emotion in music such as excitement, sadness, or joy. Keyboard music was written for the harpsichord, clavichord, and organ. The baroque style reached its zenith during the late Baroque, with the music of Bach, Handel, and Scarlatti.

MUSICAL CHARACTERISTICS OF THE BAROQUE ERA:

◼ Rhythm is one of the most distinctive elements, with a steady beat and regular accents.

◼ Pieces often have a compelling energy that endures until the end.

◼ Many pieces have a perpetual motion.

◼ Melodies are often made up of short phrase fragments of irregular lengths.

◼ There is continuity of rhythm: an opening phrase is often followed by a longer phrase with an unbroken flow of rapid notes.

◼ Works use recurring rhythmic or melodic patterns.

◼ Imitation between voices is common.

◼ Polyphonic texture is prevalent. This means that a melodic line in the right hand is usually combined with an equally important bass line.

◼ There might be two or three melodic lines within the same hand, each called a "voice."

◼ Ornamentation is used (trills, mordents, *appoggiaturas*, turns).

◼ Most sections of pieces end with an ornament that resolves to the last note.

◼ Usually one mood, or *affect*, is expressed in a baroque piece.

Library at Wiblingen, Germany. © David Hepler / GreatBuildings.com.

Looking at the art and architecture of the Baroque era, we notice that it is filled with action and movement. It is highly ornamented, and many things are happening at the same time, just as in baroque music. The term "Baroque" originally meant irregularly round, and something unusual or exaggerated. Can you see those elements in this picture?

What the student will learn in Volume Two:

Characteristics of the era:

J.S. Bach pieces:

Handel pieces:

Scarlatti pieces:

Helen Marlais' Practice Strategies®:

Volume Two – Intermediate through Early Advanced Repertoire

The pieces within each composer category are arranged in order of difficulty, with the least difficult pieces immediately following the short biography of the composer.

For a complete list of sources for these pieces (including BWV, HWV, and K/L numbers), see pages 110 and 111.

FJH1439

FOR THE STUDENT —
BAROQUE PERFORMANCE PRACTICE

This performance edition is intended to help guide students in performing baroque pieces on the modern-day piano, with full appreciation of its tonal resources and the range of articulation possibilities. C.P.E. Bach, one of J.S. Bach's sons, wrote an *Essay on the True Art of Playing Keyboard Instruments* in 1753. His book is still one of the best available resources for learning to play keyboard music.

Performers during the Baroque era were accustomed to following a set of rules, called musical conventions, which were appropriate and tasteful. These rules were applied to four basic musical points — tempo, dynamics, articulation, and ornamentation.

Tempo
Choosing an appropriate tempo helps to set the overall mood of the piece. Rhythm is perhaps the most distinctive element of baroque music, so keeping a steady beat with regular accents is extremely important.

Dynamics
Composers rarely wrote dynamic markings in their works for two reasons: The instruments of the day did not have a large dynamic range, and they trusted the performer to know the style and play accordingly. Therefore, it is up to the performer playing on a modern-day instrument, to add dynamics that show contrast within a work, that balance the character or mood of the piece, and that are stylistically appropriate. It is important to avoid excesses in crescendos and decrescendos in baroque music. Look instead to the texture, harmonies and ornamentation in each piece to decide the dynamics.

Articulation refers to how notes are attacked, accented, sustained, and phrased. In baroque keyboard literature, each note must be articulated with the best possible clarity. This book and recordings give you suggestions on how to interpret each piece. Phrasing is the creation of a musical line, and notes are grouped into phrases, just as words are grouped into sentences. Composers rarely wrote articulation or phrase markings in their works because the performance practice of the day was generally understood. For example, during the Baroque era, the instruments did not permit much dynamic change, so performers would use breaks in the sound to create accents and give the illusion of dynamics.

Today, we can use more dynamics and a greater range of articulations, so our approach can be different but appropriate for the same music. Here is a simple rule to follow for adapting these pieces to the piano: quarter notes are to be played *non legato*, while eighth notes are to be played *legato*; or if the piece is made up of eighth and sixteenth notes, then the sixteenth notes are played *legato* while the eighth notes are played *staccato*. Melodic motives are often *legato*, whereas wide intervals are *non legato*. It is important that both the attack and the release of the note be well emphasized.

An example from Bach's music:

Excerpt from "Prelude in F major"

legato →   non legato →

non legato →   ← legato

Ornamentation

Ornamentation was the way baroque composers accented strong beats and also "filled out" the texture and made the sound more elaborate and grand. Even when ornaments were not written in, it was customary for the performer to add them. It was especially customary to add embellishments on the repeats of sections and at the ends of sections. The most common ornaments are:

The trill:  or ***tr***

The trill is always played on the beat, starting on the *upper* note. The trill should have a minimum of four notes.

Other options: or   or   or

The trill with termination:

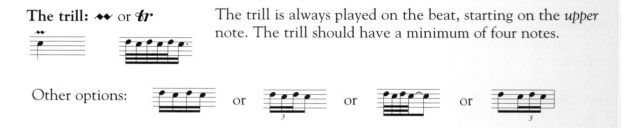

termination

Regardless of the notated time values, the termination (*Nachschlag*) is played at the same speed as the trill. The terminated trill should have a minimum of six notes.

Your choice of how to execute the trill will depend on the musical context. Examples are given in the score of each piece to help you.

The *appoggiatura*:

is played

is played

is played

The Italian word *appoggiatura* means "to lean." The *appoggiatura* is an accented dissonance played on the beat; it usually receives half the duration of the principal note. The accent is on the *appoggiatura*, and not on the principal note. This ornament should be played expressively. It gives the feeling of tension and release.

Short *appoggiaturas* are accents that are played quickly, and take very little time from the main note. These are found before a quick rhythmic group.

The *Schleifer* or slide:

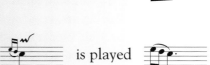 is played

is played

The slide begins on the beat and ends on the principal note. It is a two-note *appoggiatura* beginning a third below or above the main note. The slide is always played gracefully.

The mordent:

is played   or   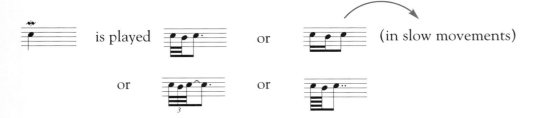 (in slow movements)

or   or

The mordent adds brilliance to notes and is always played on the beat, starting on the main note. This three-note embellishment begins on the *principal* note, goes down, and then back up. Mordents are often used in ascending melodic lines.

The turn: ∽

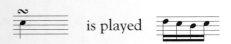 is played

The turn is added to make the music more expressive, one of the chief aims of composers during the Baroque era. The turn consists of four notes that start on the beat, beginning on the *upper* note, the main note is played, then the note below. The turn is always played as a musical extension of the melodic line.

Fingering

C.P.E. Bach began his *Essays on the True Art of Playing Keyboard Instruments* by discussing the importance of fingering: "Correct employment of the fingers is inseparably related to the whole art of performance. More is lost through poor fingering than can be replaced by all conceivable artistry and good taste."[1]

[1]William J. Mitchell, ed. and trans., C.P.E. Bach. <u>Essay on the True Art of Playing Keyboard Instruments</u>, page 41.

JOHANN SEBASTIAN BACH

(1685–1750)

When Johann Sebastian Bach was born in 1685, his musical family had been well known for more than 100 years. Members of the family were employed throughout Germany as town musicians, organists, and music directors. Most were proficient singers and played more than one instrument. When Johann Sebastian was young, he demonstrated that he had inherited the family talent. He was also a highly self-motivated student. A story is told that once, when Sebastian's older brother Johann Christoph denied him access to a book of rather difficult keyboard pieces, Sebastian waited until everyone was asleep, removed the volume, and copied the music by the light of the moon.[1] Sebastian learned to compose by copying the orchestral music of other composers, and then arranging their works for solo keyboard. He wrote out all of the music he ever composed by hand. Can you imagine writing by hand every piece in this volume?

Bach held several different positions as a music director during his lifetime, all in Germany. Unlike his contemporaries Handel and Scarlatti, who moved from country to country, Bach never left his native land.

Bach fathered twenty children. Only seven lived to be adults. Four of his sons became famous composers themselves: Wilhelm Friedemann, Carl Philipp Emanuel, Johann Christoph, and Johann Christian. When Wilhelm Friedemann turned nine in 1720, his father compiled a notebook of keyboard pieces for him. The collection is known as the *Clavier-Büchlein* ("Little Keyboard Book") *vor Wilhelm Friedemann Bach.* Over the next few years, Johann Sebastian added pieces to this notebook, including the music of some of his contemporaries whose work Bach considered significant for music instruction. Some of the pieces from the *Clavier-Büchlein* are included in this volume.

Bach held the position of Music Director in the towns of Arnstadt, Mühlhausen, and Weimar, and then became the *Kapellmeister* in Cöthen, and finally, in the city of Leipzig, was appointed Cantor, a position of great importance. During the twenty-seven years Bach worked in Leipzig, he was responsible for the musical programs in the city's four churches. For the first four or five years, he composed a new cantata every week. He wrote music for various city festivals, weddings, and funerals. He was responsible for composing all the music for the city, as well as for choosing the musicians and rehearsing the singers and instrumentalists. At the St. Thomas School, he was responsible for giving musical instruction to the fifty-five students there, who sang for the weekly worship services, and at important church and town events, to earn part of their tuition. Bach also directed the town's *Collegium Musicum,* or music club, made up of many of Leipzig's fine musicians, which gave weekly concerts at the local coffeehouses. We can be certain that Bach's music was often featured at these concerts.

*Portrait of J.S. Bach by Johann Ernst Rentsch. © Angermuseum Erfurt, Germany. Photo: Constantin Beyer

Bach worked conscientiously for the glory of God and for the pleasure of his employers and students. He wrote thousands of compositions. His works for keyboard include fantasies, toccatas, preludes, variations, fugues, suites, and concertos with orchestra. One of his most beautiful pieces is the *Goldberg Variations*, a monumental keyboard masterpiece with an aria and thirty variations. His famous work, the *Well-Tempered Clavier* was the first keyboard collection to present pieces in all twenty-four keys. Bach also wrote pieces for orchestra, such as the *Brandenburg Concertos*, and solo concertos for violin and harpsichord. Most of Bach's music was written for the church: cantatas, oratorios, and masses, all of which you can learn about in your musical future!

In 1749, in declining health, Bach underwent two operations for his failing eyesight. Neither was successful, and they left him completely blind. Johann Sebastian Bach's death in 1750 marks the end of the Baroque era.

All of Bach's known works were researched and catalogued by a music scholar named Wolfgang Schmieder. The abbreviation BWV stands for *Bach Werke Verzeichnis*, or "Bach Works Catalogue," and the corresponding number identifies where in the catalogue the music is listed. When you see the word *Anhang* or the abbreviation "Anh" after the BWV number, it means the work can be found in the Catalog Appendix. When new works by Bach are discovered, such as the *Neumeister Chorales* (in 1984), they are added to the Schmieder catalogue and assigned a BWV number.

[1]Otto Bettman. <u>Johann Sebastian Bach – As His World Knew Him</u>.
    Carol Publishing Group, New York, New York, 1995, page 63.

The family home of J.S. Bach in Eisenach, Germany.
Bachhaus in Eisenach - *Sammlung Bachhaus Eisenach/Neue Bachgesellschaft e.V.*

MINUET IN E MAJOR

This minuet was written between 1723 and 1725, when Bach was working in Leipzig. During the same time period, Bach wrote his famous oratorio, the *St. John Passion* (1724). An oratorio is a work for chorus and instrumental accompaniment that is based on a religious text.

Use of the popular minuet:

Characteristics of the Baroque Era

The minuet, normally in triple meter, is an elegant dance played at a moderate to brisk tempo. The minuet evolved in tempo and style from the Baroque through the Classical eras and remained popular until the late eighteenth century.

Many baroque pieces follow either a binary or rounded binary form.

Binary

(two sections: the A section usually ends on the dominant, and the B section begins on the dominant and ends on the tonic.)

Rounded Binary

(part of the A section returns in the B section)

BINARY form:

A		B	
Tonic	dominant	dominant	tonic
I	V	V	I

Looking at the full score, this minuet has what form? Mark the A section with the letter A, and mark the B section with the letter B. If you see the A section return in your score, mark it with the letter A.

"Smart" fingering:

Practice Strategy

It is important to use the correct fingering from the very first day of practice so that your fingers and your mind know exactly which finger should play each key. Practicing hands apart will help you. Without looking at the performance score, play the first five measures of this minuet and add your own fingering. Try many different fingerings until you find the one that suits you best. Then turn the page and try the fingering that is supplied.

MINUET IN E MAJOR

Johann Sebastian Bach
BWV 817

N.B. The slurs are editorial.

Richter's Coffee Garden: Outdoor social life during the
time Bach lived in Leipzig, Germany, 1736.

PRELUDE IN C MAJOR

Characteristics of the Baroque Era

This piece seems to be in perpetual motion; predictable cadences are not often found. This is in contrast to the music of the Classical era with its simple, flowing melodies moving to predictable cadences.

Use of a *pedal point:*

Characteristics of the Baroque Era

This entire prelude is based on a *pedal point*, which is a sustained or repeated note usually in the bass. Above this pedal point other melodic parts move. In this work, the pedal points are all half notes in the bass. While you are learning the piece, listen very carefully to the pedal point, because it is the framework from which the entire piece is built.

Practice Strategy

"Blocking" is a practice strategy you can use for many repertoire pieces.

Playing the melody notes in *harmonic* formation helps you see and feel the patterns of a piece more quickly than if you tried to learn the piece note by note. Blocking also helps you to hear the harmonies of a piece easily. You can block this entire prelude, as shown below.

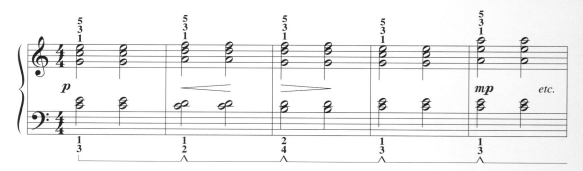

For the ending of the piece, block like this:

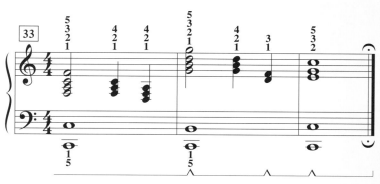

As you block all of the chords, use the pedal, and enjoy the sound of the harmonic changes throughout the piece. When playing the piece as written, you can use the pedal sparingly, like this:

Prelude in C Major

Johann Sebastian Bach
BWV 846

MINUET IN G MINOR

This minuet was written in Cöthen in 1720, when Bach was the *Kapellmeister* for Prince Leopold's court. Bach was highly productive and happy during the six years he held this position. His monumental *Brandenburg Concertos* were written two years after this minuet. Tragically, his wife, Maria Barbara, died suddenly after they had been married for twelve years. Just one year later, Bach married Anna Magdalena Wülcken, a professional singer. (You can read more about Anna Magdalena in Baroque Era, Volume One.)

This piece is found in the collection Bach compiled for his son, Wilhelm Friedemann.

Characteristics of the Baroque Era

Observe in this minuet:

- Use of a recurring rhythmic pattern
- Use of polyphonic texture

Practice Strategy

"Finger legato":

In the music of Bach, it is important to hear a *legato* line without using the pedal. In the left hand, you can strive to connect not only the bass notes, but also the tenor voice as well. Decide which fingering you like best and practice it repeatedly until it is second nature to you. Practice slowly, listening intently to make all of these connections smooth.

Measures 1 to 9, left hand:

Enjoy the splendid sound when both parts in the left hand are played *legato* without using the pedal.

MINUET IN G MINOR

Johann Sebastian Bach
BWV 842

N.B. Create a *legato* touch throughout the entire work.

PRELUDE IN F MAJOR

This prelude is one of the *Twelve Little Preludes* in the *Keyboard Book for Wilhelm Friedemann Bach*, Johann Sebastian's eldest son. At the age of nine, in 1720, Wilhelm started using this musical instruction book. This important notebook has thirty-two pieces written in it, and they were all copied by Johann Sebastian and Wilhelm. Johann helped his son learn how to copy and compose music in his own little notebook!

Characteristics of the Baroque Era

Characteristics of the Baroque era observed in this piece:

- Forward motion: In many baroque pieces, the rhythmic activity does not stop until the final chord. This kind of action is exciting to the ear because the forward motion is great.
- Use of recurring rhythmic and melodic patterns

Listen to the recording of this piece so that you can hear these musical characteristics.

Practice Strategy

Practicing back to front:

A way to work toward an excellent performance of this piece is to start with the last phrase and work backwards, adding on to it sections of the piece, working your way to the beginning. This practice strategy helps you to memorize easily by allowing you to start at different places in the music. You will feel confident that you can start at any location.

First play from the upbeat of measure 15 to the end:

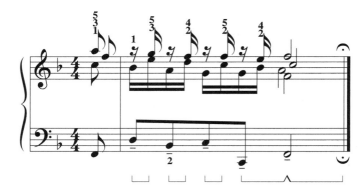

Then start at measure 12 and play to the end:

Add two to three measures each time you start, working your way to the beginning of the piece.

Prelude in F major, found in the *Keyboard Book for Wilhelm Friedemann Bach.*

The last three measures of this piece are often articulated in different ways. However, if we look at the manuscript of these measures, we see that the composer has given us clear indications of what the articulations should be. The facsimile of the manuscript above shows us that the composer placed wedges above the four sixteenth notes in the next to last bar, and then the chord is rolled for great effect.

PRELUDE IN F MAJOR

Johann Sebastian Bach
BWV 927

N.B. All eighth notes may be played detached.

PRELUDE IN C MINOR

This prelude was originally written for the lute, a popular stringed instrument of the day. Lutes are plucked, and were played from the late Middle Ages. The ancestor to European-style lutes was the Arabian 'ūd, introduced in Europe as early as the year 711! Turn to page 31 to see a picture of a Baroque lute.

Experts believe that this piece is the opening movement to a lost suite, which is why it ends on the dominant.

Characteristics of the Baroque Era

Observe in this Prelude:

■ This piece seems to be in constant motion, without any predictable cadences, except for the very end when the piece ends on the dominant. Block the left hand notes into chords, listening to how the harmonies change. You can also block the right-hand chords in the same way. The fact that the piece ends on the dominant instead of the tonic suggests that there is more to come. Maybe someday we will find the lost section of the suite!

Practice Strategy

Attention to articulations:

To create an interesting effect, throughout this piece you can make the left-hand eighth notes *staccato*. For every quarter-note downbeat, you can add a *tenuto*, which means to hold the note a bit longer, giving it slightly more emphasis:

Practice Strategy

Make every note count!

This prelude has a lively character, but if you play it too quickly, you will not be able to hear the individual notes. Articulation does not consist only of *legato* and *staccato*, but of the many subtle and fine shades in between. Be sure to play at a tempo which allows the audience to hear the subtleties of every note.

PRELUDE IN C MINOR

Johann Sebastian Bach
BWV 999

(♩ = M.M. 92–104)

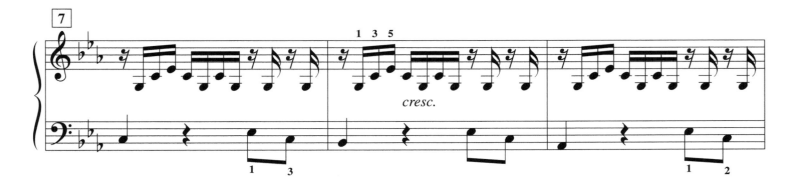

FJH1439

PRELUDE IN E MINOR

J.S. Bach explored the possibilities of the keyboard. He wrote pieces where two, three, and even four independent voices are played all at the same time. This compositional style is referred to as "counterpoint." This piece is part of a set of Bach's preludes, which he named *Five Little Preludes*.

Characteristics of the Baroque Era

Usually only one mood is expressed in a baroque piece:

This prelude should be played *legato* and have an expansive character. Listening to the CD recording of this piece, decide the single adjective from the list below that best describes the one mood of this piece. Composers during the Baroque era believed that each piece should signify a specific mood. Circle your answer below.

melancholy   *tumultuous*   *heroic*

nervous   *tender*   *cantankerous*

Practice Strategy

Improving muscle memory:

The term "muscle memory" refers to how the muscles in your fingers, hands, wrists, and arms remember the feel of the keys as each note is played. Your brain sends signals to the muscles in your body to tell them how to move. If you practice in the correct way, your muscles will learn much more quickly, and you will develop technique that is reliable even when you are nervous!

In order to learn excellent muscle memory, try the following practice strategies:

1) Divide the piece into short segments, (seven notes or less), and practice with a warm and full sound, playing solidly into the keys, with the metronome at the following speeds: eighth note = M.M. 76, and then 96.

2) To make sure that you are playing with consistent and detailed articulations, it is important that you spend part of your practice time every day playing through sections of this piece, hands apart, preferably with the metronome.

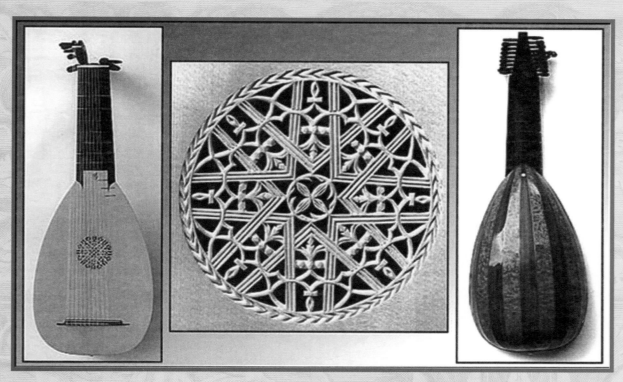

Thirteen-course baroque lute after Sebastian Schelle, 1744.
Courtesy of Stephen Barber & Sandi Harris (www.lutesandguitars.co.uk).

PRELUDE IN E MINOR

Johann Sebastian Bach
BWV 941

*The slurs from measure 1-11 are to show the long line of the phrases throughout this piece.

PRELUDE IN D MINOR

This prelude is found in the *Keyboard Book for Wilhelm Friedemann Bach.*
Johann Sebastian taught his son Wilhelm how to copy music and how
to compose. Tragically, Wilhelm's mother, Maria Barbara, passed
away shortly after this notebook was started.

**Characteristics
of the
Baroque Era**

This entire piece is created from broken chords and scale passages. This was a common way
to write pieces during this era.

**Practice
Strategy**

Playing in an improvisatory style:

In measures 39–45, we see a style of writing that is typical of the Baroque era. There is
free movement of voices, which means that broken chord patterns and scales pass freely
from one hand to another and passages may be subdivided between the hands at will.
Germans called this the "fantastic style." This is the time when you can play more
freely, as if improvising. Listen to the recording to help you understand how it can be
played.

PRELUDE IN D MINOR

Johann Sebastian Bach
BWV 926

36

N.B. Eighth notes may be played *legato*.

GAVOTTE

This work is from *French Suite Number Five*, which Bach originally included in the *Anna Magdalena Bach Notebook* of 1722.

Characteristics of the Baroque Era

■ Rhythm is one of the most distinctive elements of baroque dance music. Listen to the recording and notice that the meter is always steady and full of life.

Practice Strategy

Establishing an "inner pulse":

You can imagine that you have a conductor inside you that is consistently conducting the beat. Baroque dance music always consists of steady beats and regular accents. Here are two practice strategies that will help you succeed:

1) Listen to the recording of this and other baroque pieces, and internalize the inner pulse of the beat by moving your body from side to side. Then feel the pulse without moving. This is your sense of inner pulse. You can feel the inner pulse without moving. This is the true way to be able to add a slight *ritardando* of the beat and understand how to play this piece with real character.

2) Play the piece while counting *out loud*. Let your "inner conductor" help you. Your counting will help you with all interpretive decisions and help you perform the piece without rushing or hesitating. You may wish to try playing and counting out loud in small sections, and then larger sections, until you can play the whole piece as an entire work.

Gavotte

Johann Sebastian Bach
BWV 816

N.B. The slurs are editorial, except for those in measure 9.

MINUET IN B MINOR

This minuet is found in *Wilhelm Friedemann Bach's Notebook*. Johann Sebastian compiled this notebook for Wilhelm's lessons and used it to teach him composition. Wilhelm notated some of the pieces, while Johann copied others. Later, J.S. Bach added this minuet to his *French Suite No. 3*.

Detached-note practice:

Look at the piece and notice that two melodies are played simultaneously. This is called "counterpoint." When we use this term as an adjective we say "contrapuntal."

For any repertoire piece that is contrapuntal and has a great deal of fast passagework, here is an excellent practice strategy:

Decide with your teacher how long your practice segments will be. Then, practice with both hands playing all of the notes detached and full. Create a warm, *forte* sound. The fingers and wrists should drop fully to the bottom of the key to make a thick, full sound. Be sure to use the fingering marked in the score! This strategy helps your muscle memory, if you do it in sections of seven notes or less.

Practice with your metronome at an eighth note = 100-108:

Practice Strategy

"Impulse" practicing:

Impulse practicing begins with breaking a section of a piece into short segments, preferably seven notes or less.

Measures 17 and 18:

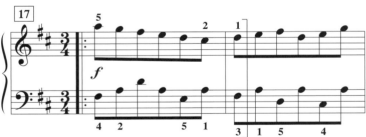

Practice Strategy

Play beats one to two, *a tempo*, listening for evenness:

This short segment played quickly, evenly, and accurately, is called an "impulse." You can expand the impulse to seven notes in a row, and then into sequential groups of seven notes together. With impulse practicing, you will find that you can play this piece and many others with wonderful agility and clarity!

MINUET IN B MINOR

Johann Sebastian Bach
BWV 929

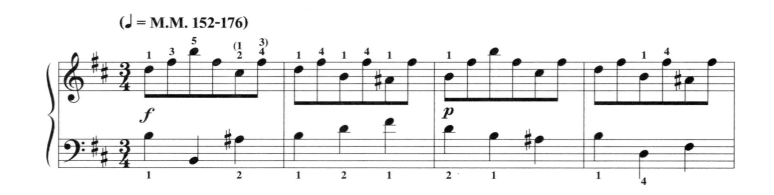

GEORGE FRIDERIC HANDEL
(1685–1759)

Born in Halle, Germany in 1685, George Frideric Handel entered this world in the same year as Johann Sebastian Bach and Domenico Scarlatti. In his teens, Handel showed himself to be a gifted keyboard player. Although his father insisted he study law, Handel studied music as well, and by the time he was seventeen he was making a living as a musician. By the age of twenty he had composed and produced his first opera.

As a young man, Handel had the good fortune of meeting Prince Ferdinando de' Medici, son and heir of the Grand Duke of Tuscany and a member of one of the most powerful families in all of Italy, sponsors of the arts for centuries. Prince Ferdinando invited Handel to live and work in Italy. With Italy the birthplace of opera, he was eager to go! In 1706, at the age of twenty-one, he moved to Rome and became employed by the Marquis Francesco Ruspoli, under whom he composed and premièred many operas. In Italy Handel visited Venice, Florence, and Naples, and met many famous Italian musicians, including Alessandro and Domenico Scarlatti, Archangelo Corelli and Antonio Vivaldi.

In 1710, Handel was appointed *Kapellmeister* (conductor) to the Elector of Hanover, who would later become King George I of England. He was given a leave of absence to travel to England, where he composed and presented the opera *Rinaldo,* a resounding success. The English loved Handel and Handel loved England in return. In 1726 he became a naturalized English citizen, anglicizing his name from Georg Friederich Händel to George Frideric Handel. In 1742 Handel composed the *Messiah,* which over the years has become one of the best-loved works in all of classical music, with its own storied traditions. It is said that at a performance of the *Messiah* in London King George II was so moved during the "Hallelujah!" chorus that he stood up; since it was customary for citizens to rise when the monarch stood, the entire audience followed. Today, it is customary, and a cherished practice, for the audience to stand during the "Hallelujah!" chorus.

Handel's fame as a composer and the success of his music helped him to amass a large fortune. He never married, concentrating instead on his writing and his career. In 1751, Handel began to lose his sight. Even though he underwent several surgeries like Bach, he was blind by the end of his life. He wrote his last works by dictating them to others. Regarded as a national treasure at the time of his death in 1759, Handel was buried in Westminster Abbey at a funeral attended by 3,000 people.

Handel was known as a humorous, generous, and honorable man with a zest for life. His music is dramatic, robust, and energetic, reflecting his personality.

*Chalk lithograph of G. F. Handel from the *Pougin Iconography Collection*, Sibley Music Library.

MINUET IN A MINOR

An extremely important characteristic of the Baroque era is the use of polyphonic texture. This means that a melodic line in the right hand is combined with at least one other equally important voice. The "continuous bass" in the left hand is just as important as the right hand.

Characteristics of the Baroque Era

"Let your right hand follow your left"
and "Left hand play out"

"Follow the leader":

Practice Strategy

Sometimes pianists get so focused on the right hand that they forget what is going on in the left hand. Let your left hand be the leader, and have your right hand follow it. Imagine that your left hand is the more important hand, and remember that the music of the left hand is what drives the rhythm and gives energy to the entire piece.

Practice sections of the piece, bringing out the left hand part. You can sing or count out loud, and imagine that a different instrument in the orchestra plays each part.

With this practice strategy you will gain confidence, and the polyphonic nature of the work will become evident.

Minuet in A minor

George Frideric Handel
HWV 549

N.B. All quarter notes should be played slightly detached.

MINUET IN G MINOR

Musical characteristics of the era exemplified in this piece:

- ■ Use of rounded binary form (see glossary for definition)
- ■ Use of recurring rhythmic and melodic patterns

**Characteristics
of the
Baroque Era**

Finger independence:

This minuet is an excellent study in learning how to independently move different fingers within the same hand. In each measure below, one of the voices must be held while the other voice plays another figure:

**Practice
Strategy**

Measures 1 to 5:

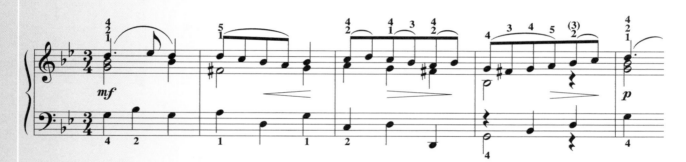

Measures 10 to 14:

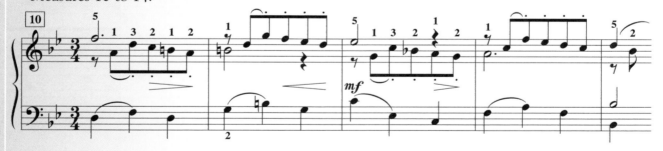

Practice very slowly, listening to be sure that each voice is held for the correct duration and that each note is carefully articulated.

Use this strategy for many similar phrases in this piece and for other baroque pieces in order to create different melodic voices within the same hand and retain the independence of the fingers.

FJH1439

MINUET IN G MINOR

George Frideric Handel
HWV 540b

N.B. Articulations are editorial in this piece.

SARABANDE

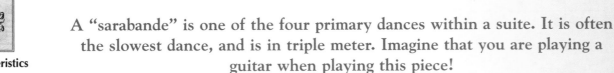

The seventeenth century has been called the "age of the variation" because variations were so popular. In variation form, a simple melody is followed by a set of movements that alter the theme. In each variation, the melody, the harmony, the accompaniment, the tempo, or the character can change.

A "sarabande" is one of the four primary dances within a suite. It is often the slowest dance, and is in triple meter. Imagine that you are playing a guitar when playing this piece!

Characteristics of the Baroque Era

Practice Strategy

To help understand variation form, look at the full score of this piece and listen to the recording.

Answer the following questions (with a pencil!):

1) Is the sarabande made up of regular or irregular phrase lengths? _____

2) Where is the melody? Mark it below by placing a line through each note that creates the melody.

3) What is the form of this piece? (ABA   ABC   AA¹A²) _____
   Each movement ends on the _____ (tonic, subdominant, dominant).

4) The sarabande is mostly (check one): homophonic _____ polyphonic _____

5) The sarabande is comprised of mostly (check one):
   broken chords _____ melody on top of blocked chords _____
   scale passages _____ arpeggios _____

6) How does the melody change in the first variation? _____

7) Which variation is the most contrapuntal? _____

8) Which variation is in chordal style, with an interesting moving melodic line in the bass? _____

9) Which variation changes the melody of the sarabande? _____

10) What is the overall mood of this piece? (check one that applies):
    jumpy   *contrite*   *regal*   *peaceful*

SARABANDE

George Frideric Handel
HWV 437

Var. 1

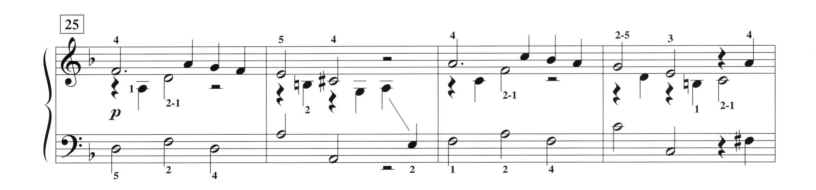

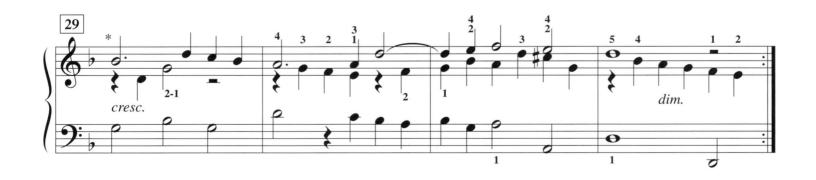

*Try substituting finger 4 for finger 5 when the G on the 2nd beat is played.

Var. 2

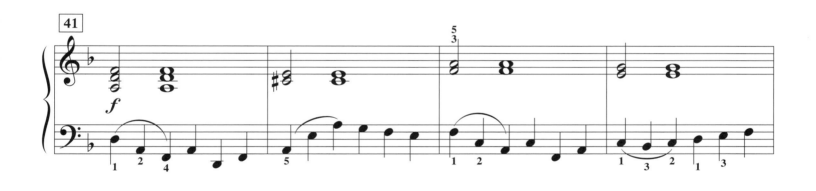

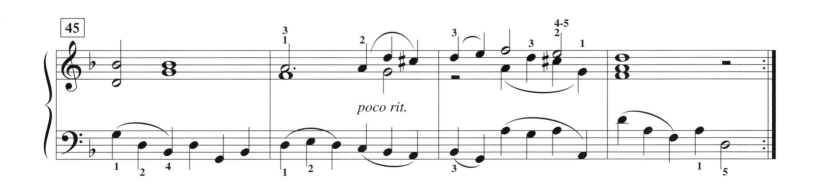

SONATINA

Characteristics of the Baroque Era

This piece displays an enduring energy.

From the beginning of the piece, there is motion that does not stop until the final measure. This kind of activity is exciting to the ear because the forward motion is great. (You can listen to the performance tracks on the downloadable recordings to hear other pieces that exhibit this same baroque characteristic.)

Practice Strategy

"Inner listening":

To understand the perpetual motion of the phrases and be able to play with ease, one must begin the mental activity of imagining what the piece should sound like. Here are a few ways to develop your musical imagination:

1) Sing the right hand melodic voice throughout the work (without the trills).

2) Sing the left hand melodic voice.

3) Start playing the piece at the beginning of different phrases.

4) Imagine which baroque instruments could play the right hand part (flute, recorder, violin), and which could play the left hand part (cello, bassoon, or viola da gamba).

5) Imagine other sounds, such as a dog barking or wind in the trees. We can hear these sounds in our imagination. If we practice, we can hear music in our imagination as well.

6) Can you listen to the music so intently in your mind that you can start playing it with a definite, solid tempo?

You can practice your "inner listening" skills away from the piano, and these will help you to achieve artistry at the keyboard.

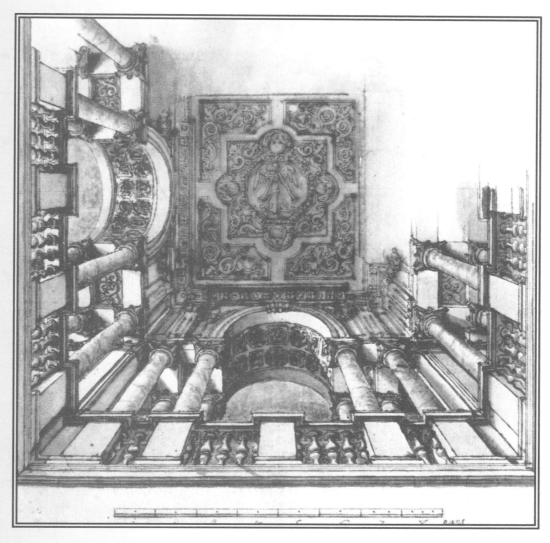

Italian Architectural design: Bolognese School.
Early 18th century architecture.

Notice the ornate baroque style of the ceiling in this room.

SONATINA

George Frideric Handel
HWV 585

PRELUDE IN F MAJOR

This particular work exists in three different versions. The first version was composed around 1717–1718. Handel revised the piece slightly in 1720, and this second version is presented in this volume. In the second version, Handel called it an "Allegro," and it was the last movement of a suite. In 1733, a third version of the piece came into being, this time in the key of G major. It is doubtful that this version was actually composed by Handel.

Characteristics of the Baroque Era

- Usually one mood is expressed in a baroque piece.
- Works use recurring rhythmic or melodic patterns.

Practice Strategy

"Unit" practicing:

This practice technique works for practically every piece you will ever play. Start with the smallest unit you are comfortable with, perhaps two beats of music. Play the notes within these beats slowly, methodically, and with correct rhythm. Repeat this "unit" many times.

Beats 1 to 2:

Then practice beats 2 to 3:

When secure, play both units without stopping:

Practicing by "units" improves muscle memory, so that your fingers, hands, wrists, and arms remember the feel of the keys as each note is played.

George Frideric Handel by Thomas Hudson.
Courtesy of the National Portrait Gallery, London.

PRELUDE IN F MAJOR

George Frideric Handel
HWV 488

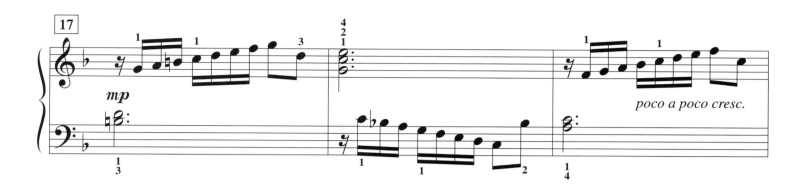

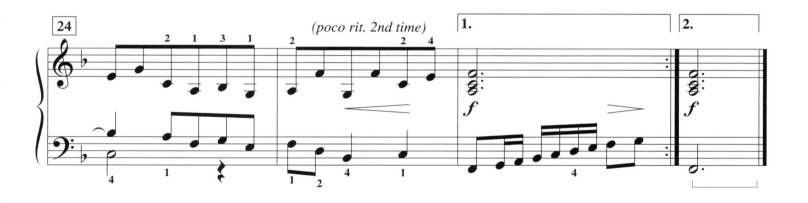

PRELUDE IN C MINOR

This prelude opens the *Partita in C minor*.

Characteristics of the Baroque Era

Look at the picture below. It shows the grandeur and magnificence that were so important during the Baroque age. Think about how this characteristic follows through not only in art and in architecture, but also in music. Therefore, by arpeggiating each chord, you will make this piece highly decorative and grand, just like the picture.

Giuseppe Galli Bibiena. Stage set of a Royal Palace.
The aristocracy was lavish in their lifestyles, as this picture suggests.

Practice Strategy

Focus on interpretation:

Use the clues that the score gives you, and listen to the sound and personality of the music as you learn this piece. Look at the full score. When the scale passages begin in measure 19, you can play them *a piacere*, which is an Italian term that means, "as you like." These scale passages can be played freely, in your own manner. You can decide the tempo, rhythm, and dynamics, so that this section sounds as though it has been improvised on the spot. We should keep our interpretations within the style of the era, and listening to the recordings can help you to absorb this sound and style. Then you will be able to create your own interpretation. Since Handel did not write in any dynamics or tempo, it is up to the performer to experiment with different interpretations and come up with the one that is best.

PRELUDE IN C MINOR

George Frideric Handel
HWV 445ª

N.B. In the Baroque era, performers would have arpeggiated the chords continuously. Since you are playing on a modern instrument with sustaining capacity, roll the chord from the bottom to the top note and let the damper pedal sustain the harmony.

ALLEMANDE

The "allemande" was typically the first movement in a Baroque suite.
Allemandes originated in the sixteenth century as a dance in duple meter.
Allemandes often start with an upbeat, and they are played at a moderate tempo.

"8 times to perfection":

Practice sections of the piece in segments of one measure plus one downbeat. Play each segment eight times in a row at a slow tempo. If it is a challenge to play an entire measure plus one downbeat, then practice a smaller segment. In order to learn pieces as well as you possibly can, make sure that you concentrate on playing the small segment with one-hundred-percent accuracy and that you play the segment eight times CORRECTLY. Once you have played the segment correctly eight times, you can practice it faster. Then put two segments together and repeat the process.

Practicing cadence points:

Another good way to make sure that you can confidently play a piece is to isolate the two cadences at the end of each section, practicing the first, then the second, and then back to the first, until you can play both easily.

Measures 7 and 8:

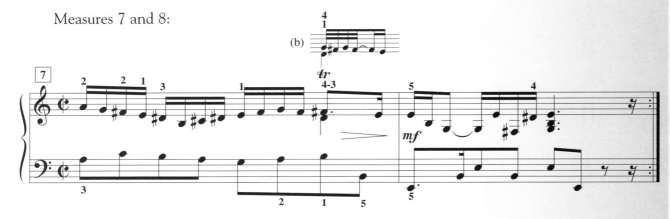

Measures 17 and 18:

Playing contrapuntal pieces with success:

Practice Strategy

1) Practice hands alone for finger independence.

2) Practice one measure plus one beat, hands alone, and then hands together.

3) Activate and energize all eighth and sixteenth notes. The energy must be felt right through you.

4) Keep a steady tempo and shape the phrase.

5) Think about the idea of constant energy and how the music and art from the era fill up space!

Baroque musician playing the flute.

Allemande

George Frideric Handel
HWV 478

View of the Gallery prepared for the reception of their Majesties, the
Royal Family, Directors, & principal Personages in the Kingdom,
at the COMMEMORATION of HANDEL in Westminster Abbey.

Commemoration of Handel at the Westminster Abbey in London, England.

SONATA

This piece was published around the year 1755, in *A Collection of Lessons* by Dr. Maurice Greene.

Pieces have perpetual motion.

During the Baroque era, pieces often seem to have few resting places. The forward motion is felt from the beginning to the end.

Take a look at both the A and B sections of this binary form sonata. When practicing, focus on the continuity of the musical line. Mark in your score with a star ★ the only two resting places in the piece.

Characteristics of the Baroque Era

Bringing a piece to life after it is learned:

Baroque composers did not add dynamic markings to their pieces. The pieces presented in this volume have some dynamic markings written in for you as a guide.

Listen to the recording and write in the dynamics that you hear for the entire piece. Add fortes, pianos, crescendos, and diminuendos, wherever you hear them. Then you can decide with your teacher if you would like to change any of these or keep them the same. Different interpretations of the same piece are intriguing to listen to. Remember it is all right to personalize your interpretation as long as it agrees with the style of the music.

Practice Strategy

What do you hear? Answer the following questions:

1) What is the dynamic level of the ending of the A section? _____

2) How is the beginning of the B section different than the beginning of the A section? _____

3) Where are the most bold and dramatic places? _____

4) Where are the quietest places? _____

5) What is the dynamic level when both hands play broken chords in measures 78–86? _____

6) What is the dynamic level of the ending of the B section? _____

Even though dynamics were limited on baroque keyboard instruments, we can use the dynamics on the modern piano to enhance and support the musical effect.

SONATA

George Frideric Handel
HHA IV/6

DOMENICO SCARLATTI

(1685–1757)

Domenico Scarlatti was born in Naples, Italy, on October 26, 1685. He came from a long line of musicians from the island of Sicily. Of his grandfather's eight children, five of them musicians, the oldest was Domenico's father Alessandro. Alessandro composed a successful opera, gaining the patronage of Queen Christina of Sweden, then living in exile in Rome, when he was only in his teens. His sudden success allowed the young man to marry just a few months before his eighteenth birthday. By the time he was twenty-four Alessandro had five children. In 1684 he moved with his family from Rome to Naples to work as Music Director and composer for the court, then ruled by the Viceroy of Spain. He and his wife had five more children there. Domenico was the oldest of the Neopolitan-born. Not much is known about Domenico's early musical training, except that his father was his teacher. He was a fine keyboard player and composer by the time he was fifteen years old, and was employed at the Neopolitan court.

From 1705–1707 Domenico lived in Venice, Italy, where he met many famous musicians, among them George Frideric Handel. The two formed a lasting friendship based on mutual respect. Handel's biographer, John Mainwaring, writes that Handel "often used to speak of Scarlatti with great satisfaction; and indeed there was reason for it; for besides his great talents as an artist, he had the sweetest temper and the genteelest behavior."[1] Scarlatti had great admiration for Handel's skills as an organist, and enjoyed his company, as well.

From Venice, Scarlatti moved to Rome, where he worked for his father Alessandro, a dominant figure in his life, and for the Queen of Poland. In 1714, Scarlatti was appointed maestro to one of the most prestigious musical establishments in all of Rome, the Cappella Giulia in the Vatican. Most of his church music was written there. He also worked for the Portuguese ambassador to the Vatican, writing music for his many social events. Alessandro managed his son's affairs, and exerted so much control over the young man's life that at the age of thirty-one, Domenico hired lawyers to force his father to grant him independence. The document releasing Domenico from Alessandro's control is still in existence.

Around 1723 Scarlatti moved to Lisbon, Portugal, and became maestro in the palace of King John V, a patron of learning and the arts. A devoted Catholic, the king built and beautified churches, and commissioned elaborate music for worship services. As part of his duties as maestro and court composer, Scarlatti gave lessons to the king's two children. The daughter, Princess Maria Barbara, proved especially gifted. She and Scarlatti developed a life-long friendship. It is believed that most — if not all — of Scarlatti's 550 harpsichord sonatas were written for her.

After Alessandro's death, Domenico, then forty-two, married a young lady twenty-seven years his junior. A few months later, in 1729, the royal families of Spain and Portugal were united by the marriage of Maria Barbara to the Spanish Crown Prince Fernando. When Maria Barbara left Portugal for her husband's home in Spain, she invited Scarlatti to accompany her. He remained in her employ for the rest of his life.

Domenico Scarlatti was one of the world's greatest harpsichord players and composers. You will find that the pieces in this volume exemplify his style well — attractive, light, agile, and colorful. His later sonatas are both technically challenging and musically brilliant. Scarlatti has been called the founder of modern piano technique. His sonatas are primarily written in single-movement *binary* form, meaning there are two sections, each repeated, with the first modulating to a related key and the second proceeding back to the tonic.

Alessandro Longo, who was from Naples, Italy, and lived from 1864 to 1945, catalogued Scarlatti's works by key, and the pieces were assigned the letter "L." Later, the influential harpsichordist Ralph Kirkpatrick (1911–1984) catalogued Scarlatti's works again, this time in chronological order, giving each piece the abbreviation "K."

[1]Malcolm Boyd. <u>Domenico Scarlatti — Master of Music</u>.
Schirmer Books, A Division of Macmillan, Inc. New York, New York, 1986, page 19.

ARIA

Practice Strategy

Slow vs. fast practicing (3 x 1 rule):

It is important to practice slowly as well as *a tempo* in order to be able to perform this piece well. Slow practice locks in the muscle memory and promotes accuracy and security, whereas *a tempo* practice encourages spontaneity, which is released in performance.

Using the 3 x 1 rule, practice short segments of the piece by playing them three times slowly (no faster than ♪ = M.M. 80), and then one time *a tempo*. Listen for absolute evenness and clarity. Begin by clapping the following rhythmic pattern:

Now clap this rhythmic pattern:

Then practice several measures in a row like this, excluding the second note of the first beat. (Turn to page 78 to see the actual piece.)

Then fill in the beats with the thirty-second notes:

Play the first thirty-second note without an accent and slightly *crescendo* to the longest note of the slur in order to shape each phrase beautifully.

Use this practice strategy on all of the phrases in order to play the rhythm correctly. You can also use the practice strategies of "eight times to perfection" and "unit" practicing to perfect your playing!

Clavichord by Chickering & Sons. Courtesy of Peter Sykes.

The clavichord was a baroque keyboard instrument played mostly in people's homes.

ARIA

Domenico Scarlatti
K. 32/L. 423

(c) Optional trill:

(c) Optional trill:

MINUET IN A MAJOR

**Characteristics
of the
Baroque Era**

Many pieces in this era use binary form.

The first section (A) begins in the tonic (I) and ends on the dominant (V). Mark (with a pencil!) a roman numeral I in the first measure of your score and a roman numeral V in the last measure of the A section. For the B section, decide which measures are tonic harmony and which are dominant. You can write either I or V below the measures.

**Practice
Strategy**

"Unit" practicing:

An easy practice strategy to use for many different kinds of repertoire is to practice by "units." A "unit" is a small segment that you and your teacher decide upon to practice repeatedly until you feel secure and comfortable with it. In this piece, a good unit would be one measure plus the next downbeat. A rule to remember is that units should be seven notes or less in each hand.

ONE MEASURE PLUS ONE DOWNBEAT
Measure one to the downbeat of measure two:

TWO UNITS TOGETHER
Measure one to the downbeat of measure three:

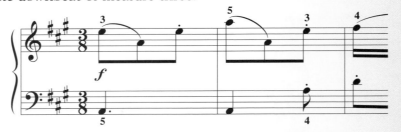

Units can be even smaller, even only two beats long, such as beats one to two! The brackets below in measures one and two show small units you can practice repeatedly:

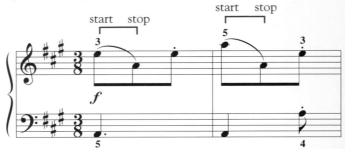

A step in the Minuet - *The Art of Dancing*
by Kellom Tomlinson, 1735.

Minuet in A major

Domenico Scarlatti
K. 83b/L.S. 31

N.B. The articulations are editorial in this piece.

SONATA IN D MINOR

This slow, one-movement work was probably written as an introduction to a violin sonata. It can be played as a solo work.

**Characteristics
of the
Baroque Era**

A copy of the sonata is shown below. This is called a facsimile because it is an exact copy of Scarlatti's manuscript, written not by Scarlatti but by a copyist during Scarlatti's lifetime. Notice the differences between the copy and the same piece on the next page. Notice the interesting marks for rests, and the numbers and accidentals that are placed above the left-hand notes. These numbers, called "figures," designated the harmonies from which an accompaniment was improvised. All keyboard players knew how to improvise from these "figures" during the Baroque era.

Facsimile of *Sonata in D minor - K. 89b*

**Practice
Strategy**

Bringing this piece to life:

This piece is introspective. Listening to the recording, mark in your score (with a pencil!) the following interpretative ideas:

1) Mark where a little extra time is taken (*poco ritardando*).

2) Mark the places where the overall sound is very quiet.

3) Is there any point where the left hand is louder than the right hand?

4) Mark the longest phrases in the piece.

Now, play only the left hand and create a long, sustained musical line. Remember to play in the same manner when adding your right hand.

SONATA IN D MINOR

Domenico Scarlatti
K. 89b/L. 211

(a) Optional trill:

SONATA IN E MINOR

This sonata is found in the manuscripts from Venice. (Please see page 106 for more information.) This set consists of fifteen volumes! The earliest, dated 1742, contains sixty-one pieces and the second volume of 1749 contains forty-one pieces. This particular piece marked *Grave* is the first of four (Grave, Allegro, Grave, Allegro), which the musicologist and harpsichordist Ralph Kirkpatrick catalogued.

Characteristics of the Baroque Era

Characteristics of the era exemplified throughout this piece:

■ Usually one mood, or *affect*, is expressed in a baroque piece.

Listen to the recording and choose one adjective from the list below that best describes this piece, and then think about this term each time you practice the piece.

fluid   *sad*   *anxious*   *joyful*

■ Melodies are usually made up of short phrase fragments of irregular lengths. An opening phrase is often followed by a longer phrase with an unbroken flow of rapid notes.

Notice in this piece that three fragments create one long phrase. This is often the case in baroque music. The first two phrase fragments are short, whereas the third phrase fragment is long. Shown below are two long phrases built upon three phrase fragments (two short, one longer). Both long phrases lead to cadence points. You can mark the rest of the phrases in the full score.

Shaping phrases:

Practice Strategy

Practice the two long phrases shown on page 86, listening to the two short phrase fragments followed by one long phrase fragment. Play in a *cantabile* style, which means in a "singing" manner. Always listen to yourself as you play, producing the most beautiful sound you can possibly achieve. This piece will be beautiful if you sustain the melodic line throughout. You can imagine each melodic note as a pearl on a string, each one beautiful and curved. It will also help you to listen to the recording.

SONATA IN E MINOR

Domenico Scarlatti
K. 81a /L. 271

SONATA IN A MAJOR

**Characteristics
of the
Baroque Era**

During the Baroque era sonatas were often written in binary form.

This form (AB) should not to be confused with the "sonata form" that became prevalent during the Classical era. (See Classical Era, Volume Two.)

**Practice
Strategy**

Complete accuracy in rhythm:

Practice all of the *appoggiaturas* in the following way:

Measure 3:   becomes:

Measure 5:   becomes:

Where else in your score do you see the same pattern?
Isolate and practice all of these patterns until they are easy for you.

Measures 24 and 61 are slightly
different from the others:

becomes:

In order to play this pattern with amazing accuracy, try the following:

1.

Practice by counting out loud and clapping this rhythm four times in a row. Use the metronome at eighth note = 160 and then quarter note = 160. Then *play* this many times.

Then:

Now add the sixteenth note and play four times in a row, with the same metronome speed.

2.

Rhythm in baroque music is vital, and this practice strategy will help you make sure that your ornaments are placed absolutely correctly!

Learning to play faster:

One of the ways to add a finishing touch is to practice with a light touch.

This practice strategy should only be applied when you can play all of the notes, rhythms, and ornaments completely in control and with complete accuracy. With the metronome, gradually increase the speed. As you do this, play more lightly and more on your fingertips. Imagine yourself playing in Baroque times on a harpsichord with a light and feathery touch. The lighter your touch, the faster you will play!

**Practice
Strategy**

SONATA IN A MAJOR

Domenico Scarlatti
K. 322/L. 483

SONATA IN D MINOR

Characteristics of the Baroque Era

Practice Strategy

Practice Strategy

Observe in this sonata:

■ Small details are repeated, changed slightly, and not just duplicated.
■ Binary form is used in baroque sonatas.

Playing expressively:

This sonata is meant to be played with feeling and sensitivity. Think about a rounded, pure tone, with clarity and warmth. Listen to the recording to hear how all of the sixteenth-note patterns as well as the dotted figures and *appoggiaturas*, are played *legato*. The forward motion is felt from the beginning to the end, with very few resting places. Listen for the supporting left-hand accompaniment that is played *non legato*, but with expression. Each note leads to the next one. This sense of musical line helps to express the emotion of the piece.

Regrouping:

Once you have learned this piece, you can use a "regrouping" practice strategy. Rather than starting at the beginning of a phrase, regroup the phrase so that it begins in different places. For example, begin playing in the *middle* of a phrase and play until you reach a downbeat. Be careful not to overly emphasize the sound of your first note by accenting it in any way. Listen to the practice strategy track as a guide.

Measure 3: Start on the second beat and play to the downbeat of measure four:

Measure 5: Again, start on the second beat and play to the downbeat of measure six:

Measure 6: Start on the third beat and play to the downbeat of measure eight:

While you play these fragments repeatedly, end the last note of the group by lifting your wrist as you lift off the key. This "regrouping" strategy makes your fingers comfortable with starting anywhere in the phrase, and will help you to gain the confidence necessary for an effective performance.

Sonata in D minor

Domenico Scarlatti
K. 77 / L. 168

(a) These short *appoggiaturas*, ♪ and ♪ are played *on* the beat, slightly accented.

FJH1439

Italian Harpsichord by Vincenzo Sodi
© 2004 The Instrumentalist Publishing Co.
Reprinted with permission from *Clavier*.

Minuet in B Flat Major

- Often, sections end with a trill.
- Works use recurring rhythmic or melodic patterns.

Characteristics of the Baroque Era

Practice Strategy

Practicing arpeggios in different rhythms will help you to achieve accuracy and build speed. You will also be able to play *leggiero*, which means playing lightly and lively.

You can also practice every note in a *detached* way, with a full sound. This can promote accuracy, since it helps you to focus on exactly which finger you use to play each key. Listen to this practice strategy on the downloadable recording to fully understand this concept.

MINUET IN B FLAT MAJOR

Domenico Scarlatti
K. 440/L. 97

N.B. The slurs are editorial.

(c) Optional trill:

(d) Optional trill:

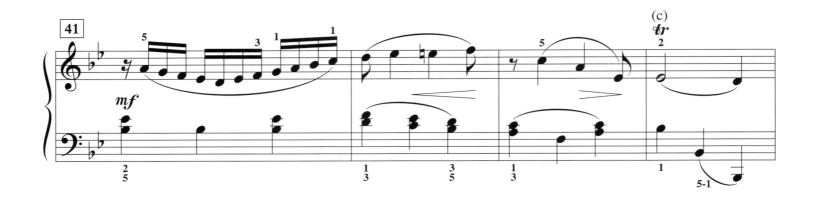

N.B. The arpeggios should be played with the right hand.

GIGUE

Not one of Scarlatti's original manuscripts has ever been found! Perhaps they were lost in one of the fires in the Spanish royal palaces. Perhaps one will be found in the future. Scarlatti's sonatas were copied in Spain, probably under the composer's supervision between 1742 and 1757. These collections of manuscripts are called the Venice and Parma manuscripts, because these Italian cities are where they are located. The Parma manuscripts are the primary source material in most cases.

A *gigue* was a popular dance during the Baroque era.
It originated in the British Isles.

Practice Strategy

Adding pedal for brilliance:

The A section of this gigue is shown below. This piece, like all of the pieces in this volume, would have originally been played on a harpsichord which did not have damper pedals like the modern piano. Since we are playing these pieces on a modern-day instrument, we can use its tonal resources. We can use the pedal sparingly throughout the work in order to add color, and to sustain a chord slightly so that it reverberates longer. The pedal has been marked for you below. Listen to the interpretation on the recording and notice where the pedal is used in moderation. Then you and your teacher can decide how much, if any, pedal you will use in this lively piece!

GIGUE

Domenico Scarlatti
K. 78/L. 75

(a) Optional trill:

(b) Optional trill:

N.B. The slurs are editorial.

FJH1439

Volume Two – Repertoire with their Sources

JOHANN SEBASTIAN BACH (1685–1750)

GEORGE FRIDERIC HANDEL (1685–1759)

(HWV = *Handel Werke Verzeichnis*, the cataloging system for Handel's works. HWV catalog numbers identify the work, regardless of where it is published. HHA = *Hallische Händel-Ausgabe*, the Halle Collected Works edition. The HHA volume numbers used for the purposes of this publication only.)

DOMENICO SCARLATTI (1685–1757)

Sources consulted for this edition:

Bach, Johann Sebastian. Die Klavierbüchlein für Anna Magdalena Bach (1722), (1725).
    Edited by Georg Von Dadelsen. Kassel: Basel: London: Bärenreiter.

Bach, Johann Sebastian. Neue Bach Ausgabe (NBA).

Bach, Johann Sebastian. Works from the Wilhelm Friedemann Bach Notebook.

Bach, Johann Sebastian. Clavierwerke, Leipzig: Breitkopf & Härtel.

Handel, George Frideric. Hallische Händel-Ausgabe (HHA).

Handel, George Frideric. The Works of George Frederic Handel. Edited by Friedrich Chrysander. Neue Ausgabe
    Sämtlicher Werke (NBA).

Handel, George Frideric. Zwanzig Klavierstücke. Edited by Willy Rehberg. Mainz und Leipzig: B. Schott's Söhne.

Handel, George Frideric. Klavierwerke IV. Edited by Terence Best. Kassel: Basel: Tours: London: Bärenreiter.

Scarlatti, Domenico. Complete Keyboard Works – in facsimile from the manuscript and printed sources.
    Edited by Ralph Kirkpatrick. New York and London: Johnson Reprint Corporation, 1972.

Scarlatti, Domenico. Le Pupitre – Collection de musique ancienne publiée sous la direction de Francois Lesure.
    Edited by Kenneth Gilbert. Paris: Heugel et Cie.

William J. Mitchell, ed. and trans., C.P.E. Bach. Essay on the True Art of Playing Keyboard Instruments,
    New York: W.W. Norton and Company, 1949.

GLOSSARY OF MUSICAL TERMS

Tempo markings

Allegro	**Allegretto**	**Moderato**	**Andante**	**Grave**
cheerful, bright, faster than *allegretto*	same feeling as *allegro*, but not as fast	a moderate tempo	walking tempo, slower than *moderato*	slow, solemn

Accompaniment – a musical background for a principal part. The accompaniment provides harmony and countermelodies for the melody.

a piacere – an Italian term that means "as you like." This means that the tempo, rhythm, and dynamics can be left up to the interpreter of the music.

Articulation – the manner of playing; the touch. Refers to how notes are attacked, and released, sustained, or accented — *legato, staccato*, etc.

a tempo – return to the regular tempo, especially after a *ritardando*.

Binary form – the structure of a piece built in two parts (AB). We label the themes as the A section and the B section. The first part sometimes ends on the tonic but most of the time ends on the dominant chord (V), and the second part begins on V and ends on the tonic. Both parts are usually marked to be repeated.

Cantabile – an Italian term for "singing." It means to play the piano in a singing style.

Countermelody – a musical line different and separate from that of the primary melody. A countermelody can serve as part of an accompaniment.

Counterpoint – two, three, four, or more melodies are played simultaneously as different voices. The harmony is implied by the melodies and the interaction of the voices. (For more information, refer to *The FJH Classic Music Dictionary*, by Edwin McLean.)

Diminuendo – to gradually become quieter; decrescendo.

Embellishment – also called ornamentation. The way composers fill out or decorate the texture, making the sound more grand.

Figured bass – numbers marked in the bass line that designated the harmonies from which an accompaniment was improvised by the performer.

Gavotte – This dance originated as a folk dance in France, becoming a popular dance of the court from the late sixteenth century to the late eighteenth century.

Homophonic texture – a melody supported by harmonies. The melodic voice is often in the right hand with chords in the left, to create the harmony. It can also be done the other way around, melody in the left hand and chords above.

Imitation – when a melodic idea is heard in one voice and subsequently heard in another voice.

Improvisation – music that is created at the exact same time it is being performed.

Kapellmeister – a German term meaning the "Chapel-master." This is a person who has the position of being in charge of all of the musical functions of a church or chapel, similar to our modern-day choir director. During the Baroque era, this was a more prestigious position than being a Music Director.

Meno mosso – an Italian term meaning "less motion" or "less quickly."

Minuet – an elegant dance in triple meter, first introduced during the time of Louis XIV in France, around the year 1650. It became a movement in the baroque suite. The dance remained popular with the upper class until the late eighteenth century.

Motive – a short melodic or rhythmic pattern (a few pitches) from which a full melodic and rhythmic phrase may grow.

(N.B.) *Nota Bene* – a Latin phrase meaning "mark well" or "take notice." Used to point out something important.

Pedal point – a bass note that is sustained while the harmonies change above it. See Bach's *Prelude in C major*.

Polyphonic texture – music with several lines (two or more) instead of a single melody and an accompaniment.

Rounded binary form – a piece in regular binary form, with one difference: the opening tune of the A section returns within the B section to lead back to a "rounded" conclusion for the piece.

Stylus fantasticus *(fantastic style)* – A free and improvisatory style, played with brilliance and flash.

Suite – a collection of dance-inspired movements that are in the same key, but are different in tempo, meter, and character. "Suite" is synonymous with the title word, "Partita."

Ternary form – music that has three sections, ABA or ABC.

Upbeat *(anacrusis)* – one or more notes in an incomplete measure occurring before the first bar line of a piece or section of music; sometimes called a "pickup."

Viola da gamba – a popular bowed string instrument with frets, usually played on the lap or between the legs, appearing in Europe towards the end of the fifteenth century and used during the Renaissance and Baroque eras.